# Cross-Stitch
## MADE EASY

Projects Designers
**Joan Green**
**Karen Nordhausen**

Contributing Writer
**Joan Green**

Publications International, Ltd.

Joan Green is a needle art designer and author of more than 60 pattern books for counted cross-stitch and plastic canvas needlepoint. She is a featured columnist for *Crafts Magazine* and is past national president of the Society of Craft Designers.

Photography by Siede/Preis Photography.

Front cover, clockwise from top left: Personal Caddy for Crayons, page 20; Vegetable Medley Napkin Holder, page 32; Decorative Jar Lids, page 10; Harvest Basket, page 16. Back cover, top to bottom: Country Welcome Plaque, page 50; Romantic Seashell Pillow, page 36; Country Quilt Swag, page 43.

Charles Craft® is a registered trademark of Charles Craft, Inc. Fray Check™ is a trademark of Dritz® Corporation. Ribband™ is a trademark of Leisure Arts. Cookin' with the "Colonel"® and Finger Lickin' Good® are registered trademarks of KFC Corporation.

The mention of products in directions is merely a record of the procedure used and is not intended as endorsement.

 # *Contents*

Introduction .........................4

Fruit Border Towel........................8

Decorative Jar Lids .......................10

American Patchwork Sampler .........12

Perky Plant Pokes ..........................14

Harvest Basket ..............................16

Calico Swags ...............................18

Personal Caddy
for Crayons ...................................20

Baby's Own Bib ...........................22

Grandma's Brood Bell Pull..............23

Home-Town Welcome
Candle Rack ................................26

Calico Apple Smock .......................28

Miniature Quilt
Dressing Screen ............................30

Vegetable Medley
Napkin Holder...............................32

Flower Lane ..................................34

Romantic Seashell Pillow ...............36

Basket of Flowers ...........................38

Kitchen Fridgies & Erasable
Memo Board.................................40

Country Quilt Swag .......................43

Butterfly Keepsake Box...................46

Chicken Lover's Potholder
and Oven Mitt ...............................48

Country Welcome Plaque...............50

Special Greeting Cards...................52

Festive Holiday Pins.......................54

Christmas Partridge Tray ...............56

Quick and Easy Christmas
Ornaments ...................................58

Noel Hand Towel...........................60

Yuletide Bell Pull & Tops for
Christmas Treats ...........................62

# Introduction

Like many needlework techniques, counted cross-stitch can be traced back centuries. It has enjoyed a strong revival in the United States for more than a decade now. Cross-stitch has evolved from the samplers of Colonial days into a stunning array of every type of design imaginable, from the very simple to pieces of extreme complexity. Talented designers have charted patterns in virtually every style and subject matter. The common lament of today's stitcher is simply that one lifetime can never hold enough hours to stitch all the patterns one would like.

It has been said that anyone who can "count," or read a chart, can do counted cross-stitch. Unlike other forms of needlecraft, counted cross-stitch consists of basically just *one* stitch—the cross-stitch, frequently accented by backstitching or outlining some areas within a design. You simply bring the needle up in one hole of the fabric, go down in another, and all of the stitches are precisely even, allowing for the perfection needleworkers find so irresistible.

Even-weave fabrics with vertical and horizontal threads of uniform thickness and spacing are used. The cloth may have as few as five threads to the inch or as many as 22 or even more, but the same design can be worked on any even-weave fabric. The only difference will be the number of strands of floss used for stitching and the size of the finished piece.

In addition to even-weave fabrics, other materials can be used for cross-stitching. "Waste canvas" is even-weave material that can be basted to sweat-shirts or other fabrics to form a grid for cross-stitching. When the cross-stitching is completed, the fabric is dampened. This allows the threads of the waste canvas to be removed, leaving only the cross-stitching. Perforated paper, perforated metal, and even baskets with a fairly even weave can be cross-stitched!

Six-strand embroidery floss is used for most stitching, and there are many beautiful metallic threads that can be incorporated as well. Another intriguing variation is working a charted design totally in beads.

Once you learn the basic cross-stitch, you can work any charted design. But for your first project, select a small design using just a few colors and stitch it on a larger-count fabric. From this you can work up to larger designs with more intricate color shading and experiment with the finer-weave or smaller-count fabrics.

One of the many advantages of counted cross-stitch is that you needn't fill in a boring background. You work only the central design, and the vast color selection of fabrics available allows you to have any color background you wish. Manufacturers have responded to consumers' needs by providing a wealth of products to entice the cross-stitcher. In addition to a large selection of even-weave fabrics in many colors and stitch counts, there are towels, bibs, afghans, garments, and Christmas socks, to mention just a few.

The list of frames and other wonderful products to accommodate the stitcher's handiwork would fill a book by itself. Visit your local needlework or craft shop to truly appreciate the marvelous variety of products available to you.

Most stitchers have often jokingly said that they're "addicted" to this fascinating hobby. So let's get started—I'll bet you can't stitch just one!

## BASIC SUPPLIES

### Fabric
The most common even-weave fabric is 14-count Aida cloth. This is an excellent choice for a beginner because its weave creates distinctive squares that make stitching very simple. Perforated paper is also 14 stitches to the inch and features pronounced, easy-to-see holes. Most of the projects in this book are worked on 14-count Aida or perforated paper.

### Needles, Hoops, Scissors
A blunt-end or tapestry needle is used for counted cross-stitch. A #24 needle is the recommended size for stitching on 14-count. An embroidery hoop may be used if desired, although it is not necessary for use on Aida cloth (and obviously would not be used on perforated paper). If you do use a hoop, be sure to remove it when not working on your piece, so that the creases will be easier to remove later. You will also need a pair of small, sharp embroidery scissors.

### Floss
Six-strand cotton embroidery floss is most often used, and it's generally cut into 18-inch lengths for stitching. Use two of the six strands for cross-stitching on #14 Aida and three strands for perforated paper. Usually one strand of floss is used for backstitching, although when stitching lettering, two strands will show up better. Refer to individual patterns for any special instructions and to the table on page 7 for the number of strands to use for fabrics of other counts.

## GETTING READY TO STITCH

### Determining Fabric Size, Cutting, and Preparation
Many patterns in this book will tell you how large the design area will be when worked on cloth of different counts, but you can calculate this yourself by taking the number of stitches across the design and dividing by the number of stitches to the inch on the fabric you are using. For example, if the design is 56 stitches across and 91 stitches up and down, and you stitch it on 14-stitch-to-the-inch cloth, the design area will be 4×6.5 inches.

The directions in this book will also tell you how large a piece you will need to make the item pictured. You can calculate this yourself, too, if you are adapting the pattern in any way. You will need to allow for a border and to protect yourself should you not get the design centered exactly. If a piece is to be framed or made into a pillow, you would probably want to add three inches or more on each of the four sides. For mini designs you can allow less. Cut your fabric evenly along the vertical and horizontal threads. You can overcast by hand or machine-zigzag the edges to prevent fraying, if desired.

### Locating Center of Design and Fabric
You can begin stitching anywhere. Fold fabric lightly in half and in half again to find the center of your piece (or measure with a ruler for perforated paper). You can begin stitching at the center. Find the center of the chart by following the arrows on the sides. You can also count up or over to another point on the chart and then count the corresponding number of squares on your cloth to find the same place.

### Reading the Chart and Beginning to Stitch
Each square on the chart represents one square of fabric or perforated paper. The colors correspond to the floss numbers listed in the color key. Select a color and stitch all of that color within an area. Begin by holding the thread ends behind the fabric until secured or covered over with two or three stitches. You may skip a few stitches to get from one area to another on the back of the material, but do not run thread behind an area that will not be stitched in the finished piece because it will show through the fabric, particularly if the floss is a dark shade. To end a strand, weave or run the thread under several stitches on the back side. Clip the ends close to the work.

Always cross all stitches in the same direction (see Figure A, page 6). For horizontal rows, work the entire row of diagonal half-stitches and then cross them coming back across the row. For vertical rows, work each complete stitch as shown in Figure B. Work all cross-stitches and three-quarter stitches (see Figure C) first. Then complete the design by working the backstitches. Follow the black lines on the graph by placing a backstitch over each weave of the fabric as shown in Figure D. If French knots are used, work these last (Figure E).

Note: It is also possible to stitch any design over two threads of the fabric. The Romantic Seashell Pillow (see page 36) is done in this fashion. Rather than use cloth with a very large count, you simply stitch the design over two threads to make it twice as large. You are actually making one stitch over a four-block area on the cloth (or two threads in each direction.) Be sure to adjust the number of strands of floss as given in the table on page 7.

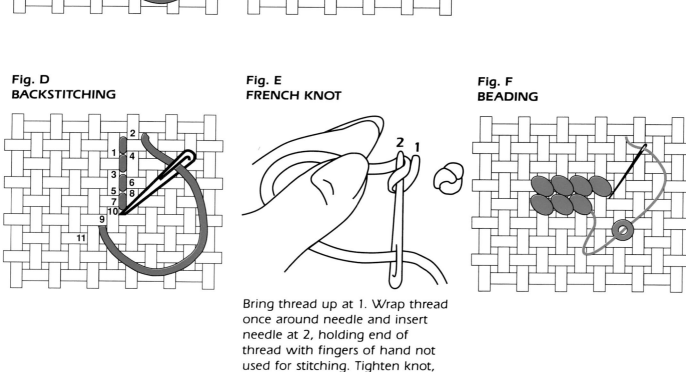

**Fig. A**
**CROSS-STITCH**

**Fig. B**
**VERTICAL CROSS-STITCH**

**Fig. C**
**THREE-QUARTER STITCHES**

**Fig. D**
**BACKSTITCHING**

**Fig. E**
**FRENCH KNOT**

**Fig. F**
**BEADING**

Bring thread up at 1. Wrap thread once around needle and insert needle at 2, holding end of thread with fingers of hand not used for stitching. Tighten knot, then pull needle through fabric, holding thread until it must be released.

## BEADING

The same charts can be used for counted beading. Small colored beads are sewn to the fabric to create the design. Use a beading needle (a very fine needle with a sharp point) and sewing thread the same color as the fabric. Each square of the chart represents a single half cross-stitch with a bead inserted over the needle and onto the thread. You can work either from left to right or from right to left, but make sure all stitches go in the same direction so that the beads lie properly.

Since you do not change thread color, work across an entire row, stitch by stitch, attaching the correct color of bead. Work from the top of the design down; do not jump more than three or four stitches without first securing the thread on the back of the work. Otherwise the last bead may be looser than the others.

Tip: To keep from losing beads or having them roll around, place a few at a time on a piece of felt and pick them up with your needle from the felt.

## CARE OF FABRIC

Try to keep your fabric as clean as possible while stitching. Should the piece become soiled, wash it gently in cold water and roll it in a towel to remove excess water. Do not twist or wring the fabric; it will leave deep creases. Press with a warm iron from the wrong side to remove wrinkles.

## SOURCES FOR SUPPLIES

Tray, arch candle rack, crayon caddy, acrylic memo board, octagonal box, thin line and crossbar frames: Wheatland Crafts, Simpsonville, South Carolina

Aida and Linaida cloth, baby bib, terry towel, potholder and oven mitt: Charles Craft, Laurinburg, North Carolina

Country Keepers, Kitchen Magnets: The New Berlin Company, Muskego, Wisconsin

Acrylic napkin holder: Personal Touch, Seffner, Florida

Dressing-screen frame: The Spinning Wheel, Milton, Wisconsin

Perforated paper, greeting cards, adhesive-backed felt, brass and wood bell-pull hardware, press-on mounting boards: Yarn Tree Designs, Ames, Iowa

Ribband™: Leisure Arts, Little Rock, Arkansas

Glue gun: Crafty Magic Melt by Ad Tech, Hampton, New Hampshire

Tacky craft glue: Aleene's (Artis Inc., Buellton, California)

Fray Check: Dritz Corporation, Spartanburg, South Carolina

| Fabric count | Number of strands | Needle size |
|---|---|---|
| #6 or #8, or #14 worked over 2 threads | 6 | 24 |
| #11 | 3 | 24 |
| #14 | 2 | 24 |
| Perforated paper | 3 | 24 |
| #18 | 2 | 26 |
| #22 (Hardanger) | 1 | 26 |

# Fruit Border Towel

Stitch a band of colorful mini fruit motifs on a towel for a bright kitchen accent. You'll think of countless ways to utilize these designs, either individually or worked in a row.

**Material used for model:**
White Estate Towel from Charles Craft

**Stitch count:**
72w × 26h

**Size:**
**#14** 5.14 × 1.86 inches

**Supplies:**
1 white Estate Towel from Charles Craft
6-strand cotton embroidery floss (see color key)
#24 tapestry needle

**Instructions:** Following the general instructions on pages 4–7, stitch according to the chart. When all cross-stitching is done, backstitch the strawberry and grape vines with dark green and backstitch the pear and pineapple with tan.

**Project options:** You can use the same design as an apron border, or try doing individual fruits on magnets or jar lid toppers.

|  |  | DMC | Bates |
|---|---|---|---|
|  | Yellow | 744 | 301 |
|  | Red | 666 | 46 |
|  | Dark red | 498 | 20 |
|  | Light green | 472 | 264 |
|  | Medium green | 989 | 242 |
|  | Dark green | 986 | 246 |
|  | Lavender | 553 | 98 |
|  | Purple | 550 | 102 |
|  | Tan | 433 | 371 |
|  | Brown | 938 | 381 |

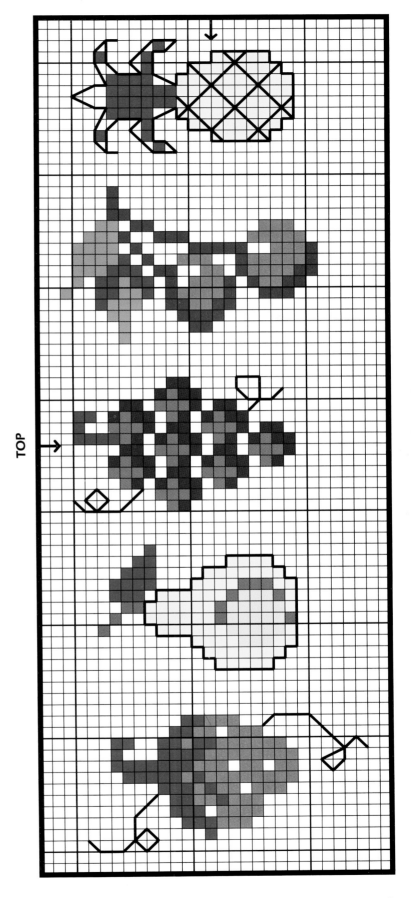

TOP

9

# Decorative Jar Lids

Stow household items and treats in these clear containers accented with clever cross-stitched lids, and you'll create true conversation pieces.

**Material used for models:**
#14 ivory Aida

**Stitch counts:**
**Buttons:** 31w×31h
**Sweets:** 43w×37h
**Scottie Dog:** 46w×46h

**Sizes:**
**Buttons:** 2.21×2.21 inches
**Sweets:** 3.07×2.64 inches
**Scottie Dog:** 3.29×3.29 inches

**Supplies:**
3 pieces #14 ivory Aida cloth,
   6×6 inches each
6-strand cotton embroidery floss
   (see color keys)
#24 tapestry needle
3 Country Keepers from The New
   Berlin Company
3 pieces calico fabric for ruffles,
   3×33 inches each (optional)

**Instructions:** Following the general instructions on pages 4–7, stitch according to the charts. Center design, leaving enough room for a seam around the edge. For Sweets, backstitch with 2 strands of gray. For Scottie Dog, stitch dog with 3 strands of black for best coverage.

To add ruffle, place stitched work in Country Keeper lid and draw a line around the outside edge of the rim. Remove work from lid. Fold one fabric strip lengthwise, wrong sides together. Baste close to the cut edges and pull thread to gather. Gather evenly to fit shape. Sew gathered strip to the

marked line with right sides together. Trim away excess Aida and overcast raw edges. Insert work into lid following manufacturer's instructions.

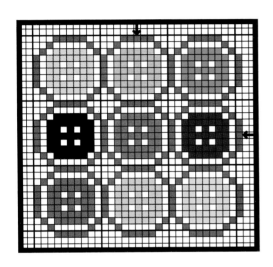

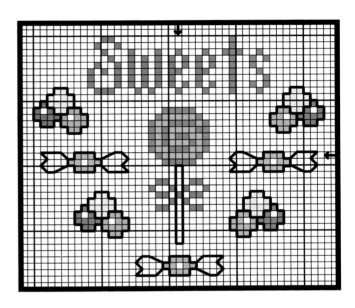

### Buttons

| | DMC | Bates |
|---|---|---|
| Pink | 224 | 893 |
| Light gray | 415 | 398 |
| Green | 703 | 238 |
| Black | 310 | 403 |
| Red | 666 | 46 |
| Brown | 801 | 357 |
| Blue | 334 | 145 |
| Tan | 437 | 942 |
| Orange | 742 | 303 |
| Dark gray | 414 | 400 |

### Sweets

| | DMC | Bates |
|---|---|---|
| Purple | 553 | 98 |
| Light pink | 604 | 55 |
| Dark pink | 601 | 63 |
| Yellow | 444 | 291 |
| Green | 700 | 228 |
| Orange | 947 | 330 |
| Gray | 414 | 400 |

### Scottie Dog

| | DMC | Bates |
|---|---|---|
| Black | 310 | 403 |
| Green | 700 | 228 |
| Light red | 666 | 46 |
| Dark red | 498 | 20 |

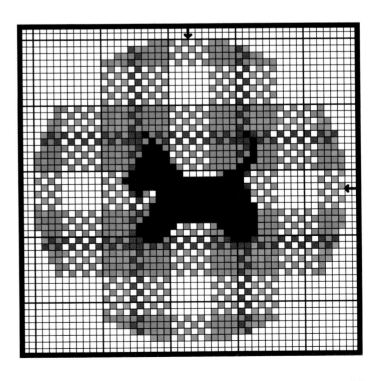

# American Patchwork Sampler

Celebrate the heartland of America with this tranquil farm scene featuring fields designed to resemble a patchwork quilt. To carry out the theme, mount it in a rustic crossbar frame.

**Material used for model:**
#14 Linaida

**Stitch count:**
93w×93h

**Size:**
**#11** 8.45×8.45 inches
**#14** 6.64×6.64 inches
**#18** 5.17×5.17 inches

**Supplies:**
1 piece #14 Linaida cloth, 15×15 inches
6-strand cotton embroidery floss (see color key)
#24 tapestry needle
10×10-inch crossbar frame

**Instructions:** Following the general instructions on pages 4–7, stitch according to the chart. When all cross-stitching is done, backstitch the stripes on the trees in dark green. Use dark brown for all other indicated backstitching. Mount in the frame following manufacturer's directions.

**Project option:** The finished piece can also be used for the face of a pillow.

| | | DMC | Bates |
|---|---|---|---|
| | Tan | 437 | 362 |
| | Light brown | 435 | 369 |
| | Medium brown | 433 | 371 |
| | Dark brown | 938 | 381 |
| | Light green | 772 | 264 |
| | Medium green | 523 | 859 |
| | Dark green | 520 | 862 |
| | Red | 347 | 13 |
| | Blue | 931 | 921 |
| | Gold | 676 | 891 |
| | Rust | 977 | 307 |

# Perky Plant Pokes

Add a little pizzazz to houseplants with these stained-glass-look hummingbird and butterfly designs—or use the more lighthearted sentiment "It's not easy being green." A cross-stitched plant poke also adds a personal touch to a plant you give as a gift.

**Material used for models:**
**Butterfly:** #14 white Aida
**Hummingbird and Frog:** #18 white Aida

**Stitch counts:**
**Butterfly:** 31w×26h
**Hummingbird:** 34w×40h
**Frog:** 38w×36h

**Sizes:**
**Butterfly: #14** 2.2×1.9 inches
**Hummingbird: #18** 1.8×2.2 inches
**Frog: #18** 2.1×2 inches

**Supplies:**
1 piece #14 white Aida cloth, 5×5 inches (for Butterfly)
2 pieces #18 white Aida cloth, 5×5 inches each (for Hummingbird and Frog)
6-strand cotton embroidery floss (see color keys)
#24 tapestry needle (for Butterfly)
#26 tapestry needle (for Hummingbird and Frog)
Iron-on backing
Florist's card holder
Fabric or felt for backing
Thick white craft glue
Rickrack, lace, or other decorative trim

**Instructions:** Following the general instructions on pages 4–7, stitch according to the charts. When all cross-stitching is done, backstitch. For Butterfly, backstitch the antenna in black and make a French knot at the end. For Hummingbird, outline the beak by backstitching in black. For Frog, outline the letters and the frog by backstitching in green.

Fuse iron-on backing to back of work. Cut out preferred shape and glue onto a card holder (obtained from a florist). Back with adhesive-backed felt or lightly glue plain felt or fabric in place. Glue desired decorative trim around the outside edge beginning and ending at the center bottom of the design.

**Project options:** Framed minis, jar lid toppers, or paperweights.

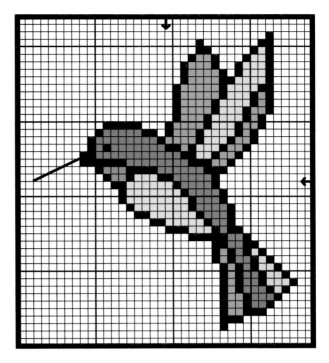

### Hummingbird

| | | DMC | Bates |
|---|---|---|---|
| | Black | 310 | 403 |
| | Red | 666 | 46 |
| | Green | 904 | 258 |
| | Light green | 906 | 256 |
| | Gold | 676 | 891 |

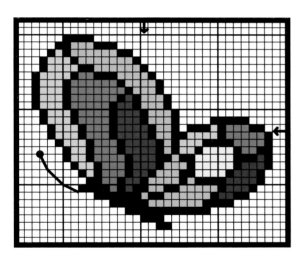

### Butterfly

| | | DMC | Bates |
|---|---|---|---|
| | Black | 310 | 403 |
| | Light aqua | 993 | 186 |
| | Aqua | 992 | 187 |
| | Dark aqua | 991 | 189 |
| | Yellow | 744 | 301 |
| | Lavender | 554 | 96 |

### Frog

| | | DMC | Bates |
|---|---|---|---|
| | Black | 310 | 403 |
| | Green | 701 | 227 |

15

# Harvest Basket

The beautiful and realistic color shading makes this basket of home-grown veggies look good enough to eat. Mount on a weathered piece of barn siding for a rustic kitchen or try a standard frame for a more traditional look.

**Material used for model:**
#14 ivory Aida

**Stitch count:**
78w×89h

**Size:**
**#11** 7.09×8.09 inches
**#14** 5.57×6.36 inches
**#18** 4.33×4.94 inches

**Supplies:**
1 piece #14 ivory Aida cloth, 10×11 inches
6-strand cotton embroidery floss (see color key)
#24 tapestry needle
Self-stick mounting board, 7½×8 inches
Thick white craft glue
1 piece weathered wood, 11×13 inches

**Instructions:** Following the general instructions on pages 4–7, stitch according to the chart. When all cross-stitching is done, backstitch the corn in red brown, the basket in dark brown, and the tomato cap in dark green. Center stitching over mounting board and affix using mounting board manufacturer's directions. Trim Aida to extend 1 inch beyond mounting board on all sides. Fold Aida around board and lightly glue in place. Glue mounted piece to wood.

| | | DMC | Bates |
|---|---|---|---|
| | Yellow | 743 | 297 |
| | Dark yellow | 742 | 303 |
| | Orange | 947 | 330 |
| | Dark red | 321 | 47 |
| | Red | 666 | 46 |
| | Very light green | 472 | 264 |
| | Light green | 470 | 267 |
| | Medium green | 937 | 268 |
| | Dark green | 890 | 879 |
| | Olive green | 3346 | 257 |
| | Red brown | 400 | 351 |
| | Very light brown | 422 | 373 |
| | Light brown | 435 | 369 |
| | Medium brown | 434 | 309 |
| | Dark brown | 938 | 381 |

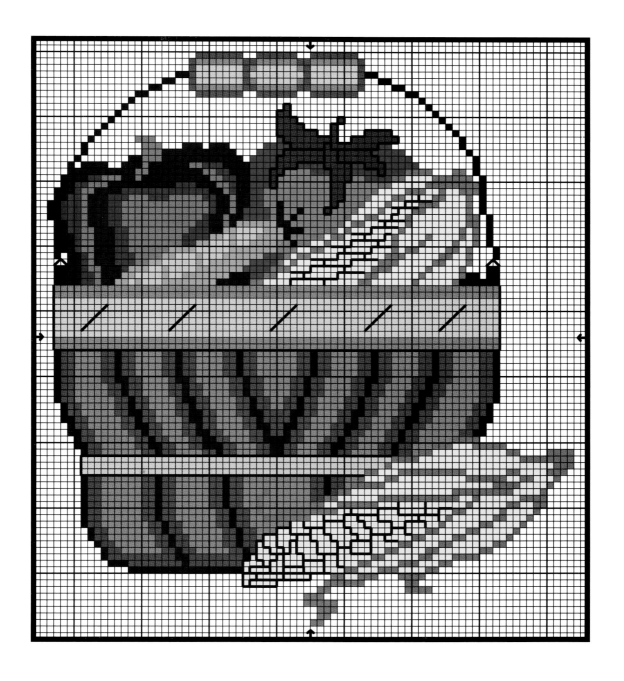

# Calico Swags

Calico cats, quilted bears, and country hearts connected with satin ribbons will make a delightful country accent for any room in the house, even the nursery! Stitching these cutout shapes on perforated paper means simple finishing and surprising durability.

**Material used for models:**
Ivory perforated paper

**Stitch counts:**
Cats: 41w×37h
Bears: 30w×41h
Large calico heart: 29w×37h
Small calico heart: 21w×19h
Large quilt heart: 30w×37h
Small quilt heart: 22w×19h

**Sizes (#14):**
Cats: 2.93×2.64 inches
Bears: 2.14×2.93 inches
Large calico heart: 2.07×2.64 inches
Small calico heart: 1.5×1.36 inches
Large quilt heart: 2.14×2.64 inches
Small quilt heart: 1.57×1.36 inches

**Supplies:**
4 pieces ivory perforated paper for cats and bears, 5×5 inches each
2 pieces ivory perforated paper for large hearts, 4×4 inches each
4 pieces ivory perforated paper for small hearts, 3×3 inches each
6-strand cotton embroidery floss (see color key)
#24 tapestry needle
Double-faced adhesive paper, if desired
1 yard ¹/₈–inch satin ribbon
Thick white craft glue
Tiny ribbon bows, if desired

**Instructions:** For cats and hearts swag, make 1 of each cat, 1 large heart, and 2 small hearts. For bears and hearts swag, make 2 bears, 1 large heart, and 2 small hearts. Following the general instructions on pages 4–7, stitch according to the charts.

For bears and hearts swag, backstitch quilting lines in dark blue. Back each piece with double-faced adhesive paper, if desired. Trim to within 1 hole of the stitching. For each swag, cut 1 piece of satin ribbon the desired length for the swag. Glue the pieces in place, spacing them about 1 inch apart. Glue tiny ribbon bows to animal necks and tops of hearts, if desired.

| | | DMC | Bates |
|---|---|---|---|
| | Rose | 224 | 893 |
| | Burgundy | 221 | 897 |
| | Medium blue | 931 | 921 |
| | Light blue | 932 | 920 |
| | Dark blue | 930 | 922 |

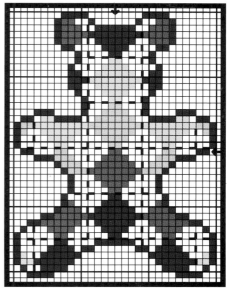

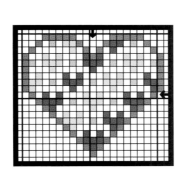

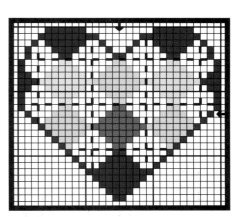

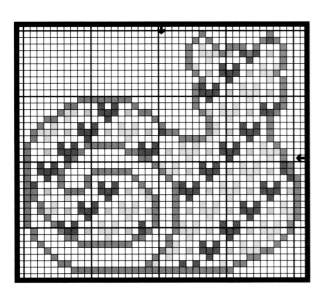

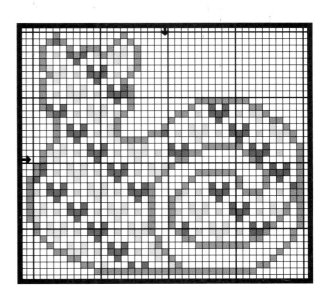

# Personal Caddy for Crayons

**Kids love crayons and coloring, so this personalized crayon caddy, with its bright and bold colored hearts, is sure to delight your favorite youngster and encourage neatness as well.**

**Material used for model:**
#14 ivory Aida

**Stitch count:**
49w×45h

**Size:**
3.5×3.21 inches

**Supplies:**
1 piece #14 ivory Aida cloth, 6×6 inches
6-strand cotton embroidery floss (see color key)
#24 tapestry needle
Wood and acrylic crayon caddy from Wheatland Crafts
Fray Check fabric fraying retardant by Dritz

**Instructions:** Use the alphabet provided to chart the desired name. Center it on the line directly above the dashed lines on the chart. The dashed lines are only to guide you in placing the name and are not to be stitched. Following the general instructions on pages 4–7, stitch according to the chart.

If desired, paint caddy base a bright color. Center stitched fabric on the sticky mounting board of the crayon caddy. To eliminate fraying, apply Fray Check to the fabric along the outside edge of the mounting board. Cut the fabric to the shape of the mounting board. With your fingers, separate the acrylic enough to slip the mounted stitching into place. To prevent breaking, do not separate the acrylic more than ¼ inch.

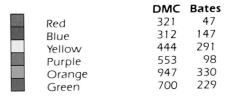

| | | DMC | Bates |
|---|---|---|---|
| | Red | 321 | 47 |
| | Blue | 312 | 147 |
| | Yellow | 444 | 291 |
| | Purple | 553 | 98 |
| | Orange | 947 | 330 |
| | Green | 700 | 229 |

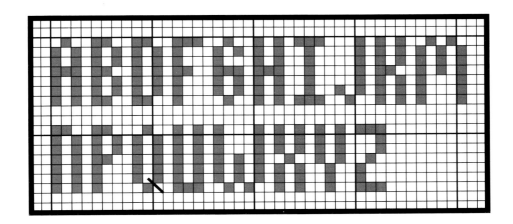

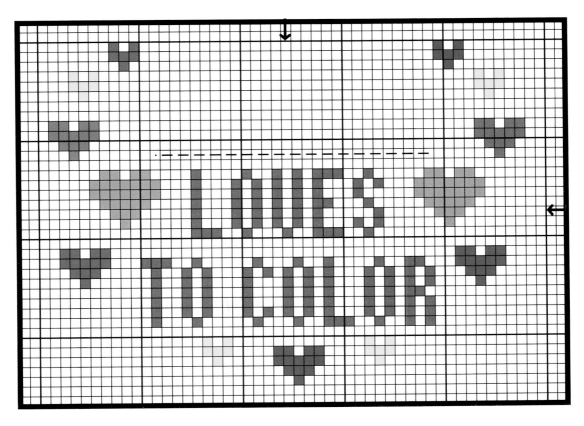

# Baby's Own Bib

The wonderful baby products with Aida bands woven right in them make stitching for baby a true delight. "Grama's Sugar 'n Spice" will be cute *and* clean wearing this super-simple terry bib.

**Material used for model:**
White terry bib from Charles Craft

**Stitch count:**
101w × 20h

**Size:**
**#14** 7.21 × 1.43 inches

**Supplies:**
1 white terry bib with Aida band from Charles Craft
6-strand cotton embroidery floss (see color key)
#24 tapestry needle

**Instructions:** Following the general instructions on pages 4–7, stitch according to the chart.

| | | DMC | Bates |
|---|---|---|---|
| | Red | 301 | 47 |
| | Dark pink | 603 | 76 |
| | Light pink | 604 | 75 |

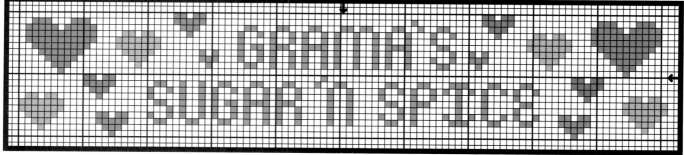

# Grandma's Brood Bell Pull

Instructions on page 24

# Grandma's Brood Bell Pull

Grandma will display this bell pull proudly! For smaller "broods," leave some eggs blank or add more eggs as needed to make room for all the grandkids.

**Material used for model:**
#14 white Aida

**Stitch count:**
52w × 174h

**Size:**
#14 3.71 × 12.43 inches
#18 2.89 × 9.67 inches

**Supplies:**
1 piece #14 white Aida cloth, 9 × 20 inches
6-strand cotton embroidery floss (see color key)
#24 tapestry needle
1 piece muslin, 9 × 20 inches
1 piece batting, 9 × 20 inches
Sharp needle
1 piece calico fabric, 10 1/2 × 21 inches
3 pieces calico fabric, 2 1/2 × 6 inches each
Decorative wooden rod

**Instructions:** Following the general instructions on pages 4–7, stitch according to the chart. Center design on Aida. Use the alphabet provided to add grandchildren's names to the eggs. When all cross-stitching is done, backstitch the lettering in red and the egg faces in brown. Do not backstitch the egg outlines at this point.

| | DMC | Bates |
|---|---|---|
| Tan | 436 | 943 |
| Red | 666 | 46 |
| Brown | 938 | 381 |

Baste stitched work to muslin with batting in between. Backstitch egg outlines with a sharp needle going through all three layers. Trim Aida, batting, and muslin to 7 1/2 x 18 inches. Lay face up on wrong side of large calico piece. Fold calico over front of Aida, folding fabric under at corners to create mitered corners.

Baste or pin in place. Fold raw edges under to create a 1-inch border of calico around stitched work. Sew mitered corners, then sew calico to Aida close to folded edges. Make calico loops from small pieces by folding each piece in half lengthwise right sides together and stitching the long edge. Turn and press so that seam

is centered on one side. Fold in half crosswise with seam out and stitch the ends together. Turn so that lengthwise seam is inside. Stitch loops to back of bell pull. Hang from wooden rod.

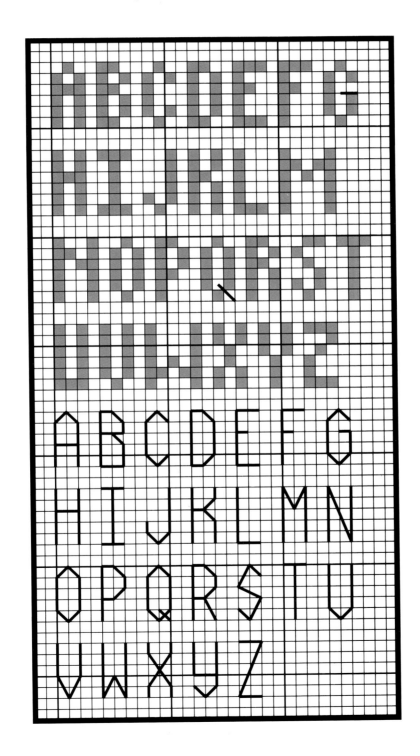

# Home-Town Welcome Candle Rack

An old-fashioned village stitched in muted country colors extends a hearty "Welcome" to your guests.

**Material used for model:**
Ivory perforated paper

**Stitch count:**
110w × 44h

**Size:**
#11  10 × 4 inches
#14  7.86 × 3.14 inches
#18  6.11 × 2.44 inches

**Supplies:**
1 piece ivory perforated paper,
   12 × 6 inches
6-strand cotton embroidery floss
   (see color key)
#24 tapestry needle
10-inch arch candle rack from
   Wheatland Crafts

**Instructions:** Following the general instructions on pages 4–7, stitch according to the chart. Mount in frame of candle rack according to manufacturer's directions.

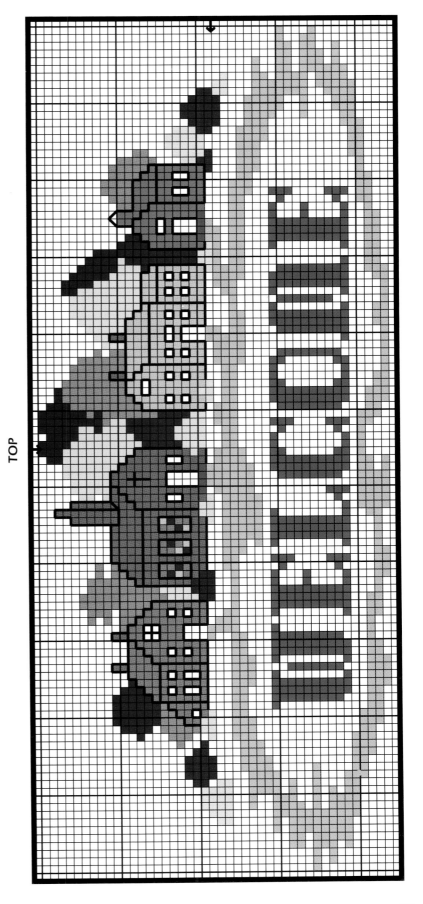

TOP

| | DMC | Bates |
|---|---|---|
| Light tan | 436 | 363 |
| Light brown | 433 | 371 |
| Dark brown | 938 | 381 |
| Rust | 920 | 339 |
| Light blue | 932 | 920 |
| Dark blue | 931 | 921 |
| Light green | 524 | 858 |
| Medium green | 522 | 859 |
| Dark green | 520 | 862 |

# Calico Apple Smock

An apple for the teacher or the cook! This colorful calico apple with tiny apples inside is perfect on a bright red apron or teacher's smock and is so quick to stitch.

**Material used for model:**
#14 white Aida

**Stitch count:**
51w×50h

**Size:**
**#11** 4.64×4.55 inches
**#14** 3.64×3.57 inches
**#18** 2.83×2.78 inches

**Supplies:**
1 piece #14 white Aida cloth,
   6¹/₂×8¹/₂ inches
6-strand cotton embroidery floss
   (see color key)
#24 tapestry needle
Smock or apron
Sewing thread to match smock
Fray Check fabric fraying
   retardant by Dritz

**Instructions:** Following the general instructions on pages 4–7, stitch according to the chart. When all cross-stitching is done, backstitch stems of small apples in dark green. Cut a 4×6¹/₂-inch oval opening in the front of the smock. Position stitched work within opening. Sew around opening from the right side using a zigzag or appliqué stitch. Trim away excess Aida on the wrong side, applying Fray Check around the edges if desired.

**Project options:** Try stitching the apple on a sweatshirt using waste canvas (see page 4).

|  |  | DMC | Bates |
|---|---|---|---|
| | Red | 666 | 46 |
| | Light green | 704 | 256 |
| | Dark green | 701 | 227 |

# Miniature Quilt Dressing Screen

Petite pastel quilts fill the panels of this dressing-screen frame. Counted quilting accents this design for an extra touch of realism and to add a dimensional effect.

**Material used for model:**
#14 ivory Aida

**Stitch count (side panels):**
41w × 45h
**Stitch count (central panel):**
39w × 41h

**Size (side panels):**
**#14** 2.93 × 3.21 inches
**Size (central panel):**
**#14** 2.79 × 2.93 inches

**Supplies:**
3 pieces #14 ivory Aida cloth, 5 × 5 inches each
6-strand cotton embroidery floss (see color key)
#24 tapestry needle
3 pieces quilt batting, 3 × 4 inches each
3 pieces muslin, 3 × 4 inches each
Sharp sewing needle
1 dressing-screen frame from The Spinning Wheel
18 inches 1¹/₂-inch gathered lace trim
1 yard ¹/₁₆-inch satin ribbon
Thick white craft glue

**Instructions:** Following the general instructions on pages 4–7, stitch the three panels according to the charts. Backstitch the letters in the central panel using 2 strands of dark rose.

To achieve the padded look, work as follows: First work the cross-stitch design. Sandwich 1 piece of quilt batting between 1 side panel and 1 piece of muslin, with the Aida on top. Baste together using long hand-basting stitches. Using 2 strands of dark rose floss and sharp needle, stitch backstitching lines through all 3 layers, knotting thread at beginning and end of each strand of floss.

To add lace trim to upper portions of frames, first glue preruffled edge of lace around inside lip of top of dressing screen. Thread ribbon onto a needle and run ribbon through bottom of lace. Pull up to gather and tie ribbon ends into a bow at the center.

To mount cross-stitching, cut mounting boards for bottom portions of frames following frame manufacturer's directions. Trim Aida, batting, and muslin to fit. Baste edges together and lightly glue to mounting board.

**Project options:** You can also frame the quilts for small pictures.

| | | DMC | Bates |
|---|---|---|---|
| | Light rose | 224 | 893 |
| | Dark rose | 221 | 897 |
| | Light green | 523 | 859 |
| | Dark green | 520 | 862 |
| | Light blue | 932 | 920 |
| | Dark blue | 930 | 922 |

# Vegetable Medley Napkin Holder

The pieces of this puzzle fit together perfectly for a striking kitchen accent. Mount in an acrylic napkin holder or stitch on larger-count fabric for a framed wall piece.

**Material used for model:**
#18 ivory Aida

**Stitch count:**
110w×92h

**Size:**
**#11** 10×8.36 inches
**#14** 7.86×6.57 inches
**#18** 6.11×5.11 inches

**Supplies:**
1 piece #18 ivory Aida cloth, 10×9 inches
6-strand cotton embroidery floss (see color key)
#26 tapestry needle
Acrylic napkin holder from Personal Touch

**Instructions:** Following the general instructions on pages 4–7, stitch according to the chart, using 2 strands of floss. When all cross-stitching is done, backstitch the large onion in medium olive; the broccoli, peas, and outer beet leaf in dark green; the pea vine in medium olive; the beet leaf veins in burgundy; the squash in light olive; the corn in medium brown; the radishes in pink red; the green onion in dark olive; the mushrooms in dark brown; and the ladybug in black. Fold Aida at all 4 edges of stitching. Insert into one side of napkin holder.

| | | DMC | Bates |
|---|---|---|---|
| | Light yellow | 745 | 300 |
| | Yellow | 743 | 297 |
| | Yellow orange | 741 | 304 |
| | Orange | 947 | 330 |
| | Red orange | 606 | 335 |
| | Dark red orange | 817 | 19 |
| | Red | 666 | 46 |
| | Burgundy | 815 | 43 |
| | Pink red | 326 | 59 |
| | Light purple | 553 | 98 |

| | | DMC | Bates |
|---|---|---|---|
| | Dark purple | 550 | 102 |
| | Light olive | 3348 | 265 |
| | Medium olive | 3346 | 257 |
| | Dark olive | 3345 | 268 |
| | Medium green | 989 | 242 |
| | Dark green | 890 | 879 |
| | Light brown | 436 | 363 |
| | Medium brown | 433 | 371 |
| | Dark brown | 938 | 381 |
| | Black | 310 | 403 |

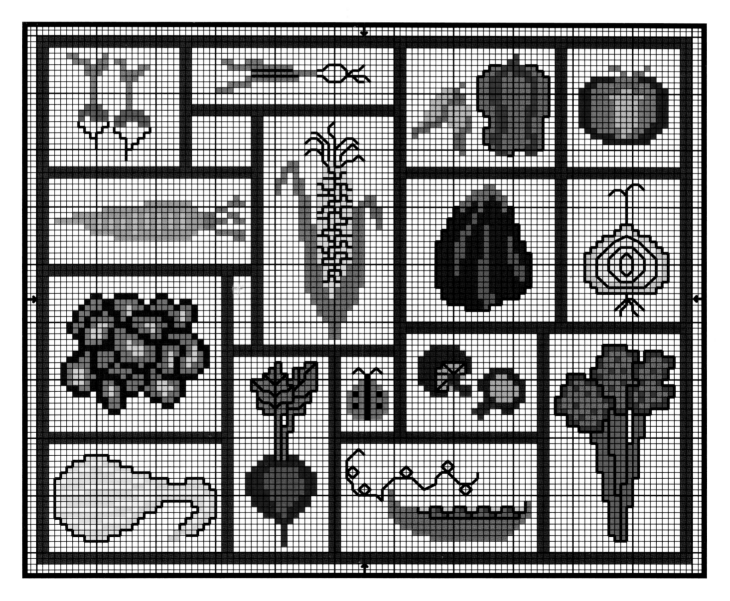

# Flower Lane

Stitch a row of stylized flowers in pretty pastels for this charming wall piece. Its checkerboard border and crossbar frame add the fresh feeling of country design.

**Material used for model:**
#14 ivory Aida

**Stitch count:**
294w×65h

**Size:**
**#14** 21×4.64 inches
**#18** 16.33×3.61 inches

**Supplies:**
1 piece #14 ivory Aida cloth, 10×27 inches
6-strand cotton embroidery floss (see color key)
#24 tapestry needle
Crossbar frame

**Instructions:** Following the general instructions on pages 4–7, stitch according to the chart. Only a portion of this chart is given. Start at the arrow on the graph, which marks the center of the design. Work two repeats to the left and two to the right as shown in the photograph of the finished design. Work the border to the edge of the frame if desired. Each flower is done in three shades of one color. You can make all flowers of the same type in the same color, or you can alternate the five color combinations as we did. To mount stitched work in frame, follow manufacturer's directions.

**Project options:** towel or apron borders, or use single flowers for small projects.

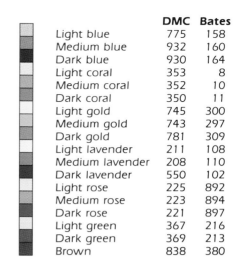

| | | DMC | Bates |
|---|---|---|---|
| | Light blue | 775 | 158 |
| | Medium blue | 932 | 160 |
| | Dark blue | 930 | 164 |
| | Light coral | 353 | 8 |
| | Medium coral | 352 | 10 |
| | Dark coral | 350 | 11 |
| | Light gold | 745 | 300 |
| | Medium gold | 743 | 297 |
| | Dark gold | 781 | 309 |
| | Light lavender | 211 | 108 |
| | Medium lavender | 208 | 110 |
| | Dark lavender | 550 | 102 |
| | Light rose | 225 | 892 |
| | Medium rose | 223 | 894 |
| | Dark rose | 221 | 897 |
| | Light green | 367 | 216 |
| | Dark green | 369 | 213 |
| | Brown | 838 | 380 |

# Romantic Seashell Pillow

A grouping of delicate seashells worked in subtle shades and sewn into a pretty, lace-trimmed pillow makes a lovely accent for a bedroom.

**Material used for model:**
#14 ivory Aida (stitched over two threads)

**Stitch count:**
80w × 80h

**Size:**
**#11** 7.27 × 7.27 inches
**#14** (over 2) 11.43 × 11.43 inches
**#14** 5.71 × 5.71 inches
**#18** 4.44 × 4.44 inches

**Supplies:**
1 piece #14 ivory Aida cloth, 14 × 14 inches
6-strand cotton embroidery floss (see color key)
#24 tapestry needle
48 inches eyelet lace
12 × 12-inch pillow form
14 × 14-inch piece plain fabric (for pillow back)

**Instructions:** Following the general instructions on pages 4–7, stitch according to the chart. Use 6 strands of floss and stitch over 2 threads. When all cross-stitching is done, backstitch the coral with rust, using 6 strands. Backstitch nautilus shells with tan, using 3 strands. Backstitch wave border with aqua, using 6 strands. Backstitch other shells with dark brown, using 3 strands.

To make pillow, sew lace to outer edge of right side of Aida with the lace facing toward the center of the design. Begin and end at the center bottom of design. Pin stitched Aida and pillow backing right sides together. Sew, using 1/2-inch seam allowance and leaving a 6-inch opening at center bottom for turning. Trim excess fabric from corners, cutting diagonally across each corner close to stitching. Turn pillow right side out, insert pillow form, and whipstitch opening.

|  | DMC | Bates |
|---|---|---|
| Light peach | 754 | 778 |
| Dark peach | 758 | 868 |
| Ivory | 712 | 926 |
| Light violet | 3042 | 869 |
| Dark violet | 3041 | 871 |
| Khaki | 612 | 832 |
| Rust | 356 | 5975 |
| Light brown | 842 | 376 |
| Medium brown | 840 | 379 |
| Dark brown | 839 | 360 |
| Tan | 433 | 371 |
| Gray | 318 | 399 |
| Gold | 725 | 306 |
| Aqua | 964 | 185 |

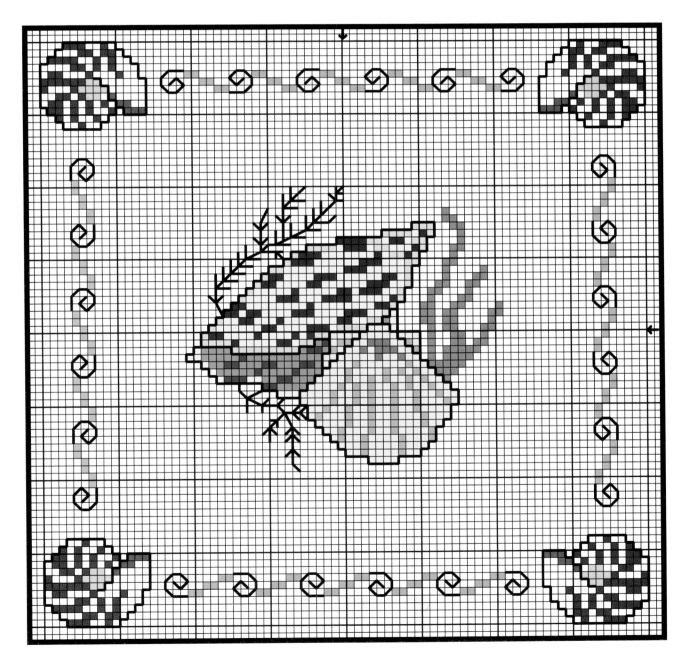

# Basket of Flowers

The freshness of these spring flowers in their white wicker basket stands out prominently against the dark background cloth used for this striking piece—a truly classic look.

**Material used for model:**
#14 brown Aida

**Stitch count:**
135w×82h

**Size:**
**#14** 9.64×5.86 inches
**#18** 7.5×4.55 inches

**Supplies:**
1 piece #14 brown Aida cloth, 14×9 inches
6-strand cotton embroidery floss (see color key)
#24 tapestry needle
12×18-inch picture frame with oval mat

**Instructions:** Following the general instructions on pages 4–7, stitch according to the chart. When all cross-stitching is done, backstitch the inside hyacinths in dark green. Do all remaining backstitching in brown. Mount finished work in frame following manufacturer's directions.

**Project options:** Try stitching this on a dark blue background or other dark-colored fabric.

| | DMC | Bates | | | DMC | Bates | | | DMC | Bates |
|---|---|---|---|---|---|---|---|---|---|---|
| Ivory | 712 | 387 | Dark purple | 333 | 119 | Light yellow | 744 | 301 |
| Brown | 938 | 381 | Palest coral | 353 | 6 | Medium yellow | 743 | 297 |
| Light green | 989 | 266 | Light coral | 352 | 8 | Dark yellow | 742 | 303 |
| Dark green | 987 | 268 | Coral | 351 | 10 | Yellow orange | 741 | 304 |
| Lavender | 341 | 117 | Medium coral | 350 | 11 | Orange | 740 | 316 |
| Purple | 340 | 118 | Dark coral | 349 | 13 | | | |

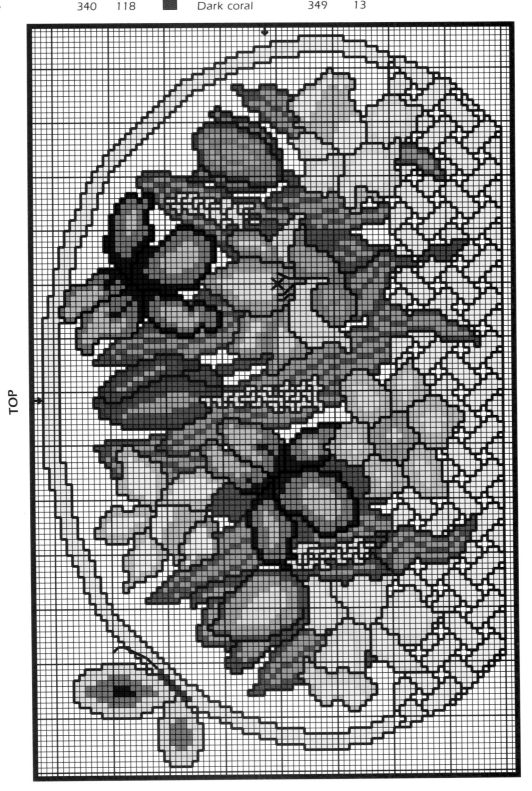

TOP

# Kitchen Fridgies & Erasable Memo Board

Instructions on page 42

These super-simple fruits and veggies stitch up in no time and are easy to mount in colored heart-shaped magnets.

**Material used for models:**
#14 white or ivory Aida

**Stitch count:**
19w × 18h

**Size:**
1.36 × 1.29 inches

**Supplies:**
1 piece #14 white or ivory Aida cloth, 3 × 3 inches, for each magnet
6-strand cotton embroidery floss (see color key)
#24 tapestry needle
Kitchen Magnets from The New Berlin Company

**Instructions:** Following the general instructions on pages 4–7, stitch according to the charts. Mount in kitchen magnets following manufacturer's directions.

| | | DMC | Bates |
|---|---|---|---|
| | Red | 666 | 46 |
| | Green | 701 | 227 |
| | Orange | 740 | 316 |
| | Yellow | 742 | 303 |
| | Brown | 898 | 360 |

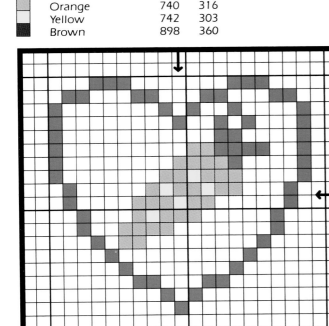

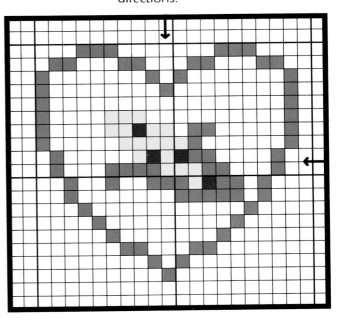

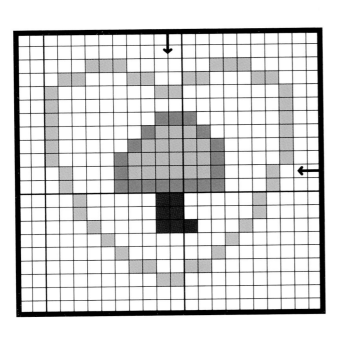

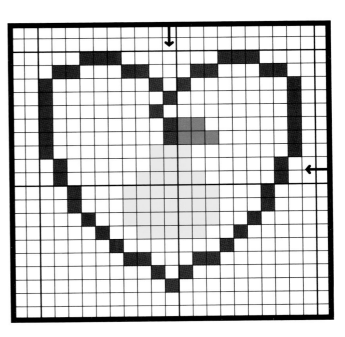

# Erasable Memo Board

Get organized with this magnetic memo board for your refrigerator. The acrylic board comes with its own pen, and messages wipe off easily with a dry cloth.

**Material used for model:**
#18 white Aida

**Stitch count:**
97w×24h

**Size:**
5.39×1.33 inches

**Supplies:**
1 piece #18 white Aida cloth,
   8 ×10 inches
6-strand cotton embroidery floss
   (see color key)
#26 tapestry needle
5×7¹/₂–inch acrylic note board
   from Wheatland Crafts
Thick white craft glue
Fray Check fabric fraying
   retardant by Dritz

**Instructions:** Following the general instructions on pages 4–7, stitch according to the chart. When all cross-stitching is done, backstitch the vines in green and the blossoms in yellow.

Center stitched work on the sticky mounting board from the note board. Trim Aida to extend ³/₄ inch beyond mounting board on all sides. Fold to back and glue lightly in place. With your fingers, separate the acrylic just enough to slip the mounted stitching into place. To avoid breaking, do not separate the acrylic more than ¹/₄ inch.

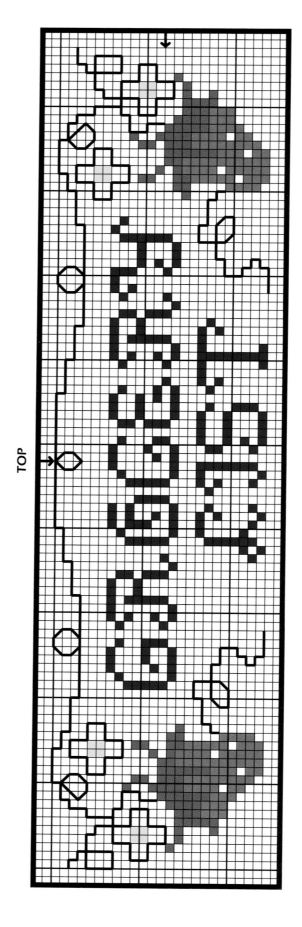

TOP

| | | DMC | Bates |
|---|---|---|---|
| | Yellow | 444 | 291 |
| | Red | 666 | 46 |
| | Green | 3346 | 257 |
| | Dark green | 890 | 879 |

# Country Quilt Swag

Instructions on page 44

# Country Quilt Swag

If you don't have an antique quilt to hang on your wall, just stitch up this trio of miniature quilts. Hang them from a piece of twine or other cording, securing them with petite clothespins, and you'll have a darling country wall swag.

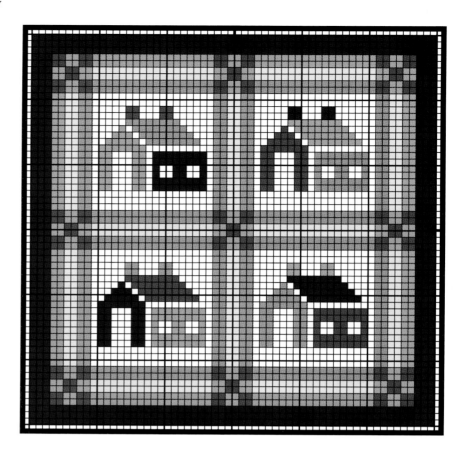

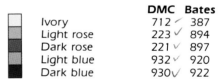

| | | DMC | Bates |
|---|---|---|---|
| | Ivory | 712 | 387 |
| | Light rose | 223 | 894 |
| | Dark rose | 221 | 897 |
| | Light blue | 932 | 920 |
| | Dark blue | 930 | 922 |

**Material used for model:**
Brown perforated paper

**Stitch count (each quilt):**
60w×60h

**Size (each quilt):**
#14 4.29×4.29 inches

**Supplies:**
3 pieces brown perforated paper,
  6×6 inches each
6-strand cotton embroidery floss
  (see color key)
#24 tapestry needle
1¹/₂ yards twine, string, or cording
6 miniature wooden clothespins

**Instructions:** Following the general instructions on pages 4–7, stitch according to the chart. Use 3 strands of floss for cross-stitching. On the Star Quilt, backstitch quilting lines using 2 strands of dark rose. On the Flower Basket Quilt, backstitch quilting lines using 2 strands of dark blue.

When stitching is completed, trim any excess paper, leaving just one unworked row around each side. Overcast the edges of each quilt using 6 strands of floss and making 1 stitch for each square. Make 2 or 3 stitches at each corner for best coverage. Overcast the House Quilt using light rose, the Star Quilt using dark rose,

and the Flower Basket Quilt using dark blue. Arrange the three quilts on twine using clothespins.

**Project options:** You can also frame the quilts for small pictures.

| | | DMC | Bates |
|---|---|---|---|
| | Ivory | 712 | 387 |
| | Light rose | 223 | 894 |
| | Dark rose | 221 | 897 |
| | Light blue | 932 | 920 |
| | Dark blue | 930 | 922 |

# Butterfly Keepsake Box

A glorious beaded butterfly graces the lid of this attractive box—what an elegant gift for someone special. An alternate project features a blue butterfly sewn into a velvet evening bag.

**Material used for model:**
#14 ivory Aida

**Stitch count:**
51w×47h

**Size:**
3.64×3.36 inches

**Supplies:**
1 piece #14 ivory Aida cloth, 7×7 inches
Mill Hill glass beads (see color keys)
Beading needle
Ivory sewing thread
Metallic gold thread
6-inch octagonal box from Wheatland Crafts

**Instructions:** Following the instructions for beading on page 7, stitch according to the chart. Backstitch the antennae with metallic gold thread, making a French knot at the end of each antenna. Mount in box lid following manufacturer's directions.

For blue butterfly, backstitch antennae with 2 strands DMC 823 (navy) floss blended with 1 strand of Kreinik blending filament 085 (peacock), making a French knot at end of each antenna. Inset into velvet drawstring bag as desired.

**Project options:** Try cross-stitching the design in your favorite colors and mounting in a frame with a circular mat.

### Pink version

| | Mill Hill Bead |
|---|---|
| Pink | 145T |
| Old rose | 553T |
| Violet | 206T |
| Old gold | 557T |
| Copper | 330T |

### Blue version

| | Mill Hill Bead |
|---|---|
| Light blue | 146T |
| Sapphire | 168T |
| Iris | 252T |
| Antique silver | 556T |
| Rainbow | 374T |

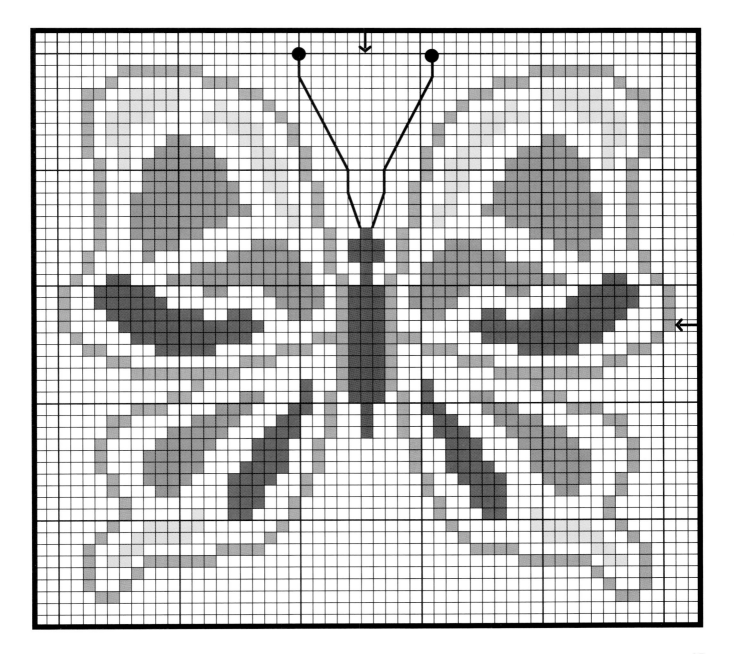

# Chicken Lover's Potholder and Oven Mitt

This potholder and oven mitt duo are a must for all chicken lovers. "Cookin' with the Colonel" and "Finger Lickin' Good" provide a touch of whimsy and are easy to stitch on prefinished kitchen items.

**Material used for models:**
White potholder and oven mitt from Charles Craft

**Stitch counts:**
**Cookin':** 60w×21h
**Finger:** 50w×21h

**Sizes:**
**Cookin': #14** 4.29×1.5 inches
**Finger: #14** 3.57×1.5 inches

**Supplies:**
1 white potholder from Charles Craft
1 white oven mitt from Charles Craft
6-strand cotton embroidery floss (see color key)
#24 tapestry needle

**Instructions:** Following the general instructions on pages 4–7, stitch according to the charts. When all cross-stitching is done, backstitch in brown the quotation marks around "Colonel," the apostrophe after "lickin'" and "Cookin'," and around the chickens.

| | | DMC | Bates |
|---|---|---|---|
| | Orange | 349 | 13 |
| | Rust | 922 | 338 |
| | Brown | 938 | 381 |
| | Dark rust | 920 | 339 |

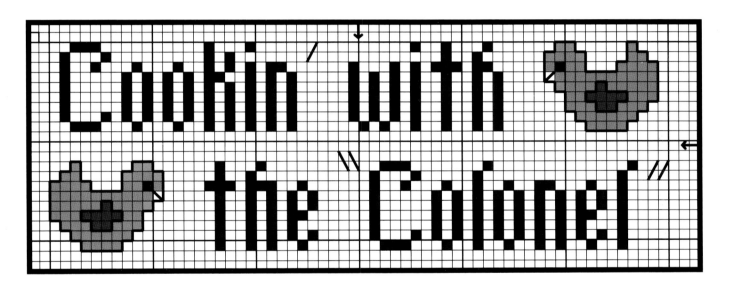

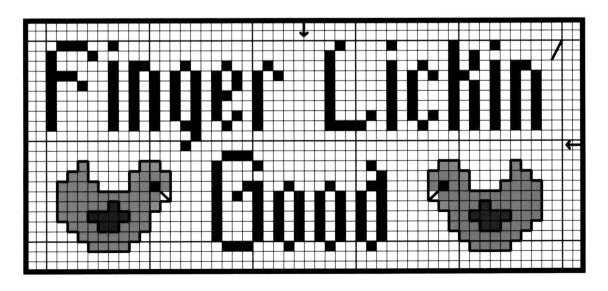

# Country Welcome Plaque

**Versatile perforated paper becomes a stitched mat for this country-inspired wall piece. Cut a heart and two sunbonnet girls out of the paper and mount your favorite shade of calico behind it. Another good combination would be rose calico and hearts and a country blue checkerboard border.**

**Material used for model:**
Brown perforated paper

**Stitch count:**
101 w × 97 h

**Size:**
**#14** 7.21 × 6.93 inches

**Supplies:**
1 piece brown perforated paper, 9 × 12 inches
6-strand cotton embroidery floss (see color key)
#24 tapestry needle
1 piece burgundy calico fabric, 9 × 12 inches
9 × 12-inch thin-line oak frame from Wheatland Crafts

**Instructions:** Begin cross-stitching 4 inches from top edge, making sure design is centered from side to side. Following the general instructions on pages 4–7, stitch according to the chart. Use satin stitch for the brown letters. Place cutout designs on wrong side of perforated paper with bottom edge of cutout ³/4 inch from top cross-stitching line, making sure designs are centered over stitching. Trace cutout designs onto wrong side of perforated paper. Cut out with small, sharp scissors. Mount perforated paper over calico fabric in frame according to manufacturer's directions.

| | DMC | Bates |
|---|---|---|
| Brown | 3371 | 382 |
| Burgundy | 815 | 43 |
| Green | 520 | 862 |

# Special Greeting Cards

Easy to stitch and mount in special blank cards, these cross-stitched sentiments are sure to delight the recipient.

**Material used for models:**
**New Baby:** #14 ivory Aida
**Anniversary:** #14 white Aida
**Birthday:** White perforated paper
**Wedding:** #18 white Aida

**Stitch counts:**
**New Baby:** 22w×38h
**Anniversary:** 17w×25h
**Birthday:** 35w×36h
**Wedding:** 29w×29h

**Sizes:**
**New Baby: #14** 1.57×2.71 inches
**Anniversary: #14** 1.21×1.79 inches
**Birthday: #14** 2.5×2.57 inches
**Wedding: #18** 1.61×1.61 inches

**Supplies:**
1 piece #14 ivory Aida cloth, 5×7 inches (for New Baby)
1 piece #14 white Aida cloth, 5×7 inches (for Anniversary)
1 piece white perforated paper, 6×8 inches (for Birthday)
1 piece #18 white Aida cloth, 5×7 inches (for Wedding)
6-strand cotton embroidery floss (see color key)
#24 tapestry needle
#26 tapestry needle (for Wedding)
3 greeting cards from Yarn Tree Designs, 4×6 inches each (for Baby, Anniversary, and Wedding)
1 greeting card from Yarn Tree Designs, 5×7 inches (for Birthday)
Glue

**Instructions:** Following the general instructions on pages 4–7, stitch according to the charts. Half-colored squares represent three-quarter stitches (see page 6). When all cross-stitching is done, backstitch where indicated. For New Baby, backstitch lettering with aqua and stork with gray. For Anniversary, backstitch lettering, bells, and clappers with dark gold. For Birthday, backstitch lettering with brown and candle flames with orange. For Wedding, backstitch lettering with dark rose.

Trim the completed project to fit the opening in the center of the card. Use a small amount of glue or a glue stick to tack the project to the card. Apply a small amount of glue around the edge of the card and close the card. Place the card under a book to dry.

### Anniversary

| | | DMC | Bates |
|---|---|---|---|
| | Light gold | 725 | 306 |
| | Dark gold | 782 | 308 |
| | Blue | 931 | 921 |

### New Baby

| | | DMC | Bates |
|---|---|---|---|
| | Aqua | 958 | 187 |
| | Orange | 740 | 316 |
| | Black | 310 | 403 |
| | Gray | 414 | 400 |
| | Light pink | 3326 | 25 |
| | Dark pink | 961 | 76 |

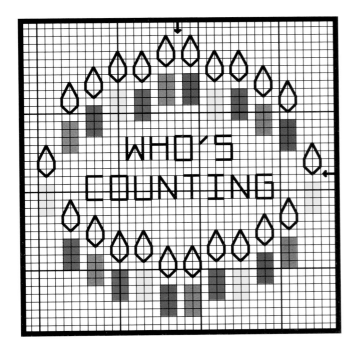

### Birthday

| | | DMC | Bates |
|---|---|---|---|
| | Yellow | 973 | 290 |
| | Orange | 740 | 316 |
| | Red | 666 | 46 |
| | Green | 700 | 229 |
| | Blue | 312 | 147 |
| | Brown | 938 | 381 |

### Wedding

| | | DMC | Bates |
|---|---|---|---|
| | Light rose | 223 | 894 |
| | Dark rose | 221 | 897 |
| | Blue | 931 | 921 |

# Festive Holiday Pins

Put some sparkle into Halloween and Christmas with an assortment of counted beadwork scatter pins. Sew the beads directly on perforated paper and follow the easy finishing instructions.

**Material used for models:**
White or ivory perforated paper

**Stitch counts:**
**Jack-o'-Lantern:** 21w×20h
**Ghost:** 20w×24h
**Santa:** 23w×24h
**Angel:** 25w×18h

**Sizes:**
**Jack-o'-Lantern:** 1.5×1.43 inches
**Ghost:** 1.43×1.71 inches
**Santa:** 1.64×1.71 inches
**Angel:** 1.79×1.29 inches

**Supplies:**
1 piece white or ivory perforated paper, 3×3 inches, for each pin
Mill Hill glass beads (see color keys)
Sewing thread to match perforated paper
Beading needle
1 piece adhesive-backed paper or fabric, 3×3 inches, for each pin
Glue gun or thick white craft glue
1 bar pin for each pin

**Instructions:** Following the beading instructions on page 7, sew on beads according to the charts. Affix beaded design to adhesive-backed paper or fabric.

Trim both the perforated paper and the backing to within one square of the finished design. Glue a bar pin to the back side of the design.

**Project options:** magnets or jar lid toppers.

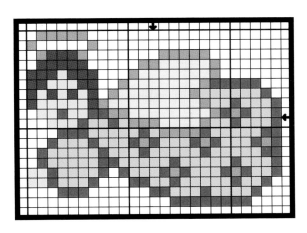

### Angel

| | | Mill Hill Bead |
|---|---|---|
| | Old gold | 557T |
| | Copper | 330K |
| | Pale peach | 148T |
| | Christmas red | 165T |
| | Pink | 145T |
| | Crystal | 161T |

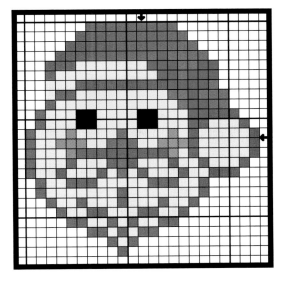

### Santa

| | | Mill Hill Bead |
|---|---|---|
| | Christmas red | 165T |
| | Christmas green | 167T |
| | Jet | 81T |
| | White | 479K |
| | Pale peach | 148T |
| | Old rose | 553T |
| | Gray | 150T |

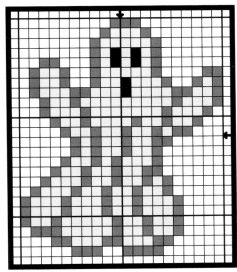

### Ghost

| | | Mill Hill Bead |
|---|---|---|
| | Gray | 150T |
| | White | 479K |
| | Jet | 81T |

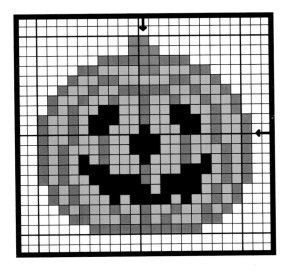

### Jack-o'-Lantern

| | | Mill Hill Bead |
|---|---|---|
| | Jade green | 431 |
| | Christmas red | 165T |
| | Tangerine | 423 |
| | Jet | 81T |

# Christmas Partridge Tray

Serve your guests in style with this beautiful wooden tray with its holiday motif. Rich jewel-tone colors highlight this rendition of the familiar Christmas song.

**Material used for model:**
#11 white Aida

**Stitch count:**
113w×88h

**Size:**
**#11** 10.27×8 inches
**#14** 8.07×6.29 inches
**#18** 6.28×4.89 inches

**Supplies:**
1 piece #11 white Aida cloth, 14×16 inches
6-strand cotton embroidery floss (see color key)
#24 tapestry needle
9×12-inch rectangular tray from Wheatland Crafts (overall dimensions 13×16¹/₂ inches)

**Instructions:** Following the general instructions on pages 4–7, stitch according to the chart. Fill in unmarked areas inside black border with aqua. Mount in tray using manufacturer's directions.

**Project options:** The finished piece can also be framed as a wall picture.

|  | | DMC | Bates |
|---|---|---|---|
| | Black | 310 | 403 |
| | Gold | 725 | 306 |
| | Light green | 704 | 255 |
| | Dark green | 701 | 227 |
| | Magenta | 917 | 89 |
| | Lavender | 554 | 90 |
| | Purple | 552 | 101 |
| | Aqua | 807 | 168 |

# Quick and Easy Christmas Ornaments

Cross-stitched Christmas ornaments are always welcome. These traditional designs in their petite golden frames would be particularly appropriate for a tabletop tree.

**Material used on models:**
#14 white Aida

**Stitch counts:**
**Snowman:** 16w×17h
**Angel:** 12w×16h
**Santa:** 12w×14h
**Horn:** 14w×12h
**Drum:** 13w×11h
**Tree:** 12w×16h

**Sizes:**
**Snowman:** 1.14×1.21 inches
**Angel:** .86×1.14 inches
**Santa:** .86×1 inch
**Horn:** 1×.86 inch
**Drum:** .93×.79 inch
**Tree:** .86×1.14 inches

## Supplies:

6 pieces #14 white Aida cloth, 3×3 inches each
6-strand cotton embroidery floss (see color key)
#24 tapestry needle
6 small gold-colored frames, each with 1¹/₂-inch openings

**Instructions:** Following the general instructions on pages 4–7, stitch according to the charts. Half-colored squares represent three-quarter stitches (see page 6). When all cross-stitching is done, backstitch where indicated.

**For Snowman,** backstitch hat, brim, and mouth with 2 strands of black. Backstitch scarf and eyes with 1 strand of black. Use French knots in black for nose and buttons. Backstitch sticks with 2 strands of dark tan.

**For Angel,** backstitch halo with 2 strands of yellow. Backstitch wings with 1 strand of gray. Backstitch nose and mouth with 1 strand of brown. Backstitch dress and heart with 1 strand of burgundy.

**For Santa,** backstitch cap with 1 strand of burgundy. Backstitch eyes with 1 strand of black. Backstitch all other lines with 2 strands of gray.

**For Horn,** backstitch horn with 1 strand of dark tan and backstitch notes with 1 strand of black.

**For Drum,** backstitch lines on drum with 2 strands of yellow. Use French knots in yellow for ends of lines. Backstitch drumsticks with 2 strands of black and use French knots in black for the ends.

**For Tree,** backstitch star with 2 strands of yellow.

Trim each ornament to fit in frame. Mount in frame according to manufacturer's directions.

**Project options:** Stitch on larger-count cloth for larger ornaments and jar lid toppers.

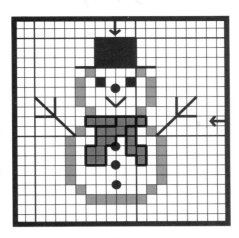

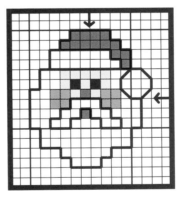

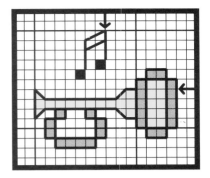

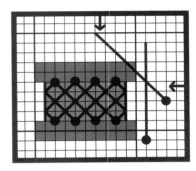

### Horn and Drum

| | DMC | Bates |
|---|---|---|
| Yellow | 725 | 306 |
| Light tan | 436 | 363 |
| Dark tan | 434 | 309 |
| Black | 310 | 403 |
| Emerald | 700 | 228 |
| Red | 666 | 46 |

### Snowman, Angel, and Santa

| | DMC | Bates |
|---|---|---|
| Yellow | 725 | 306 |
| Dark tan | 434 | 309 |
| Flesh | 754 | 4146 |
| Pink | 604 | 50 |
| Gray | 414 | 400 |
| Black | 310 | 403 |
| Red | 666 | 46 |
| Burgundy | 815 | 44 |
| Emerald | 700 | 228 |

### Tree

| | DMC | Bates |
|---|---|---|
| Emerald | 700 | 228 |
| Red | 666 | 46 |
| Yellow | 725 | 306 |
| Pink | 604 | 50 |
| Brown | 898 | 360 |

# Noel Hand Towel

Spell out "Noel" in a red and green Christmas plaid for a special touch in your bathroom. Cross-stitch the design on Ribband™ and sew to a velour hand towel in rich green or red.

**Material used for model:**
Ivory Maxi Weave Ribband™

**Stitch count:**
98w × 20h

**Size:**
**#14** 7 × 1.43 inches

**Supplies:**
18 inches ivory Maxi Weave
  Ribband™
6-strand cotton embroidery floss
  (see color key)
#24 tapestry needle
1 red or green velour hand towel

**Instructions:** Following the general instructions on pages 4–7, stitch according to the chart. Center the design on the width of the towel about 2 inches from one edge. Sew Ribband to towel along edges of Ribband.

**Project options:** Stitch the letters vertically for a bell pull or stitch either horizontally or vertically for a place mat.

TOP

| | | DMC | Bates |
|---|---|---|---|
| | Red | 666 | 46 |
| | Green | 701 | 227 |

# Yuletide Bell Pull & Tops for Christmas Treats

**Instructions on page 64**

**If Christmas makes you dream of hot cocoa, home-baked cookies, and plum pudding, you'll want this bell pull to hang for the holidays. Stitched on large-count cloth and trimmed with colorful gingham, it makes a bold statement about the joys of Christmas cooking for your kitchen.**

**Material used for model:**
#8 white Aida

**Stitch count:**
30w×252h

**Size:**
**#8** 3.75×31.5 inches
**#11** 2.73×22.91 inches
**#14** 2.14×18 inches
**#18** 1.67×14 inches

**Supplies:**
1 piece #8 white Aida cloth, 8×36 inches
6-strand cotton embroidery floss (see color key)
Calico or gingham fabric, 8×36 inches
2 yards jumbo rickrack
Brass bell-pull hardware from Yarn Tree Designs

**Instructions:** Following the general instructions on pages 4–7, stitch according to the chart. For #8 Aida, use 6 strands of floss. Note that the bell pull is worked all in one piece. To fit it into the book, the chart was broken down into three sections. At the top of the second and third sections, we have reprinted part of the wording at the end of the previous section to aid in placement.

When all cross-stitching is done, backstitch lettering, bread, plum pudding, outside and mouth of gingerbread boy in dark brown. Backstitch candy jar and steam in gray. Backstitch cookies and cups in medium brown. Backstitch candy canes, suit on gingerbread boy, red line on ribbon candy, and zigzag line on bell cookie with red. Backstitch black line on ribbon candy with green.

Trim finished piece to 5¹/₂×30 inches. Lay fabric over stitched work, right sides together. Sew fabric to stitched work at the bottom. Turn and press. Fold sides of fabric over front of stitched piece to form ¹/₂-inch border; trim fabric to fit. Pin or baste rickrack over edge of fabric; sew. Sew fabric to Aida at the top without turning fabric under. Trim fabric to 7¹/₂ inches wide and 2¹/₂ inches from top of Aida. Fold under ¹/₂ inch on all three sides; sew. Fold to back of work over bell-pull rod; sew to tack in place.

|  | DMC | Bates |
|---|---|---|
| Yellow | 725 | 306 |
| Red | 666 | 46 |
| Green | 701 | 227 |
| Light brown | 781 | 309 |
| Medium brown | 433 | 371 |
| Dark brown | 938 | 381 |
| Gray | 414 | 400 |

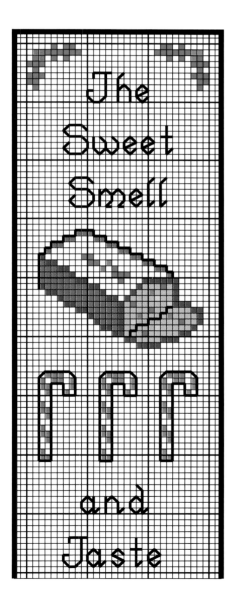

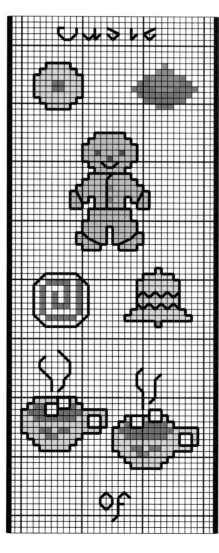

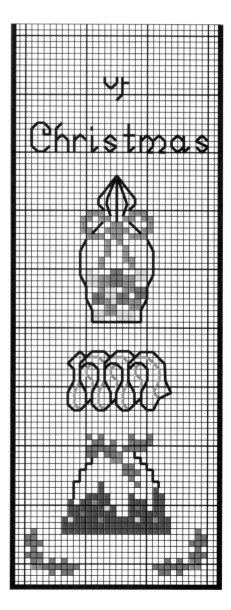

# Tops for Christmas Treats

Holiday confections will look especially enticing when you display them in these containers topped with colorful Christmas motifs. And presenting your homemade goodies in one of these will make a truly thoughtful holiday gift.

**Instructions:** Following the general instructions on pages 4–7, stitch according to the charts. Center design, leaving enough room for a seam around the edge. When all cross-stitching is done, backstitch. For Yule Yummies, backstitch peppermint stick with red. Backstitch red lines on ribbon candy with red and black lines with green. Use long, straight stitches with red for small candy centers. Use red French knots for holly berries. For Christmas Quilt, backstitch lines with red.

If a ruffle is desired, place stitched work in Country Keeper lid and draw a line around the outside edge of the rim. Remove work from lid. Fold one fabric strip lengthwise, wrong sides together. Baste close to the cut edges and pull thread to gather. Gather evenly to fit shape. Sew gathered strip to the marked line with right sides together. Trim away excess Aida and overcast raw edges. Insert work into lid following manufacturer's instructions.

**Material used for models:**
#14 ivory Aida

**Stitch counts:**
Yule Yummies: 32w×38h
Christmas Quilt: 53w×51h

**Sizes:**
Yule Yummies: 2.29×2.71 inches
Christmas Quilt: 3.79×3.64 inches

**Supplies:**
2 pieces #14 ivory Aida cloth, 6×6 inches each
6-strand cotton embroidery floss (see color keys)
#24 tapestry needle
2 Country Keepers from The New Berlin Company
2 fabric strips for ruffles, 3×33 inches each (optional)

### Christmas Quilt

|  |  | DMC | Bates |
|---|---|---|---|
|  | Red | 666 | 46 |
|  | Light green | 700 | 229 |
|  | Dark green | 890 | 879 |

### Yule Yummies

|  |  | DMC | Bates |
|---|---|---|---|
|  | Red | 666 | 46 |
|  | Dark red | 498 | 20 |
|  | Green | 700 | 228 |